PRAYERS

God Always Answers

For Healing

Publications International, Ltd.

INTRODUCTION

Sickness, disability, heartsickness, grief: our lives are marked by events that weaken our spirits and our bodies. Our best life experiences — having families, taking risks, making ourselves vulnerable — can cause stress and pain even as they lift us up. Prayer gives each of us a direct line to God when we need it most, whether for our long-term ailments and troubles or fleeting moments of sickness. He always answers our prayers; we need to learn to hear him.

And ye shall serve the Lord your God, and he shall bless thy bread, and thy water; and I will take sickness away from the midst of thee.

— *Exodus 23:25*

Many of Jesus's miracles involve healing, and the Bible contains almost countless examples of God's statements about illness or pain. In Exodus, and this verse in particular, we see the promise of healing and the requirement that we serve God in order to receive that healing. Inside this book, you'll find examples of all forms of healing: physical, emotional, and spiritual. In time, you'll find that while God is listening the same as he always was, you're more prepared to listen.

T he Lord watch between me and thee, when we are absent one from another.

— Genesis 31:49

We all know the sting of being heartsick. Loss, unrequited love, unfulfilled expectations—any of these can lead to the feeling of our heart literally being sick. God knows the pain we experience in this life. He knows how to comfort us. If we cling to hope and turn to God, despite all that life may throw at us, we are sure to find ourselves filled with peace and joy.

He will swallow up death in victory; and the Lord God will wipe away tears from off all faces.

— *Isaiah 25:8*

May your thoughts focus much more upon what you have than what you lack in this trying time. May your heart lay hold of present realities rather than future possibilities. For this moment—the now—is in front of us. Whether we are sick or healthy, this juncture in time is the place we share. Let us be blessed in this moment, safe in our knowledge of God's plan for us. Let us simply be in God's presence, just for this moment.

For the Lord God will help me;
therefore shall I not be confounded:
therefore have I set my face like a flint,
and I know that I shall not be ashamed.

— Isaiah 50:7

There are many events in our lives over which
we have no control. However, we do have
a choice either to endure trying times and
press on or to give up. The secret of survival,
whether or not we question God's presence or
His ability to help us, is remembering that our
hope is in the fairness, goodness, and justice of
God. When we put our trust in the character
of a God who cannot fail us, we will remain
faithful. Our trust and faithfulness produce
the endurance that sees us through the "tough
stuff" we all face in this life.

A man's pride shall bring him low: but honour shall uphold the humble in spirit.

— Proverbs 29:23

Ready or not, free time is at hand for some of your finest seasoned workers, Lord, early retirees downsized, out-sized, and put prematurely out to pasture. Help us start again, for we are hidden treasures other companies could use. Remind us as we start the search that even temporary employment is better than sitting around. Keep us in the workforce, for we, like fine furniture, gain luster with age, something young folks can't begin to match.

*N*ow faith is the substance of things hoped for, the evidence of things not seen.

— *Hebrews 11:1*

My heavenly Father, what do I have to fear when you are the one caring for me? And yet, I do fear; irrationally I fear, despite your faithfulness, despite your assurances, and despite your promises. Why do I still fear? I don't always understand my trembling heart and the shadows of things far smaller than you before which it cowers. Please liberate me from these lapses of trust. Free me to stand fearlessly, supported by faith and hope, in the center of your great love for me.

*L*ittle children, yet a little while I am with you. Ye shall seek me: and as I said unto the Jews, Whither I go, ye cannot come; so now I say to you. A new commandment I give unto you, That ye love one another; as I have loved you, that ye also love one another.

— John 13:33–34

The simplest idea can be the most challenging to really do. On our busiest days, we must love one another. In our most trying times, we must still love one another. With no caveats or excuses, we must always love one another. We can work to make this love easier to find in ourselves by being appreciative, grateful, and humble during our best times — stockpiling those feelings like a rainy-day fund.

Hear the right, O Lord, attend unto my cry, give ear unto my prayer, that goeth not out of feigned lips.

— *Psalms 17:1*

Every adult has likely seen a child tell a bad lie: "I'm too sick to go to school," or maybe "I don't know who broke the vase." There may as well be a neon sign, because most children don't have the skills that let adults tell much more convincing lies to each other. Take a minute to clear your heart of clutter before you go to God, and be honest with him and yourself.

I will pay thee my vows, Which my lips have uttered, and my mouth hath spoken, when I was in trouble.

— *Psalms 66:13–14*

Crisis bargains with God are played for laughs or tears in movies, but in real life, these prayers can help us out of some serious jams. It's important to be thankful for the help we receive, whether it's a last-minute medical miracle or simply the calm we need to face the day.

For this cause we also, since the day we heard it, do not cease to pray for you, and to desire that ye might be filled with the knowledge of his will in all wisdom and spiritual understanding.

— *Colossians 1:9*

Paul's love and fellowship shines through in his epistles where he, like Christians ever since, reaches out to support people who have recently heard the good news. When we struggle, ache, and suffer, our fellows surround us and help us to heal. Relationships and community can strengthen the fortress of faith more than almost anything else.

*A*nd shall not God avenge his own elect, which cry day and night unto him, though he bear long with them? I tell you that he will avenge them speedily.

— Luke 18:7–8

The unjust judge in the Gospel of Luke gives in and rules in the widow's favor. He doesn't realize he is the vehicle for her answered prayers. Jesus Christ tells the story to show how true faith prevails even from the least likely source.

B ehold, I will bring it health and cure, and I will cure them, and will reveal unto them the abundance of peace and truth.

— *Jeremiah 33:6*

Inner peace and calm are vital to health. Chronic stress weakens our immune systems and impairs our bodies and minds. When spiritual life seeks to replace illness and doubt with "peace and truth," our minds and bodies can thrive.

*A*nd therefore will the Lord wait, that he may be gracious unto you, and therefore will he be exalted, that he may have mercy upon you: for the Lord is a God of judgment: blessed are all they that wait for him.

— *Isaiah 30:18*

Patience runs in both directions between us and God. Think about the relationships in your life: there must be people you wish were more patient, but are you also patient as you wait for them to learn?

J esus healed many without resorting to miracles and seems to have resorted to the miraculous only to convince his hearers of his authority in divine matters. In some cases, as the woman who touched his garment, he claimed nothing for himself, but told her that her own faith had served her.

— *Russell H. Conwell*

F or the people shall dwell in Zion at Jerusalem: thou shalt weep no more: he will be very gracious unto thee at the voice of thy cry; when he shall hear it, he will answer thee.

— *Isaiah 30:19*

When we're faced with obstacles, it's tempting to keep trying anything and everything in our power, but then we feel hopeless if nothing works. We are never hopeless in God's power.

*B*ut now, O Lord, thou art our father; we are the clay, and thou our potter; and we all are the work of thy hand.

— *Isaiah 64:8*

Have you worked with clay? It's flexible, strong, and almost impossible to ruin. God is the potter, but we, the clay, must hold our shape and endure. If we're marred, the flaws can be smoothed.

In the day of my trouble I sought the Lord: my sore ran in the night, and ceased not: my soul refused to be comforted.

— Psalms 77:2

The darker Psalms serve an important purpose by giving us an outlet when our own souls refuse to be comforted. We want to cry or scream in frustration until we feel ready to return to God.

I f my people, which are called by my name, shall humble themselves, and pray, and seek my face, and turn from their wicked ways; then will I hear from heaven, and will forgive their sin, and will heal their land.

— 2 Chronicles 7:14

We pray in desperate or troubling times, and these prayers can include promises to give up a bad habit or behavior. Why wait for a trial in order to make a pledge to God?

Read the Psalms through, making careful record of all the statements of what the Lord was to the writers of the Psalms. The list will surprise you. Then on your knees go over them one by one, with the prayer that Christ may be to you what he was to David and the others.

— Rosalind Goforth

The idea is foolishly unrighteous which looks upon the arrangement of Providence as a slot machine into which the pretended worshiper may put a copper penny and draw out a gold dollar. As gold must be given for gold, so love must be given for love.

— Russell H. Conwell

To God I cried when troubles rose,
He heard me and subdued my
foes, He did my rising fears control, And
strength diffused through all my soul.

— Nancy Luce

I the Lord do keep it; I will water it
every moment: lest any hurt it, I will
keep it night and day.

— Isaiah 27:3

To nurture is a constant job. God's ever-
present attention gives us the tools we need
but we must choose to take those tools and
grow toward the sun of his love.

T hen he turned his face to the wall, and prayed unto the Lord, saying, I beseech thee, O Lord, remember now how I have walked before thee in truth and with a perfect heart, and have done that which is good in thy sight.

— *2 Kings 20:2–4*

Hezekiah's deathbed prayer foretold many of the guidelines Jesus Christ later gave to the Apostles. The prayer was short and direct, spoken humbly and in a private place. God answered Hezekiah's prayer by adding years to his life.

I s any sick among you? let him call for the elders of the church; and let them pray over him, anointing him with oil in the name of the Lord.

— *James 5:14*

Any illness is a shame, especially if a child is sick. We trust in the medicine and science God has made possible, but prayer shows both God and our loved ones how invested we are.

It may seem strange that any men should dare to ask a just God's assistance in wringing their bread from the sweat of other men's faces, but let us judge not, that we be not judged. The prayers of both could not be answered. That of neither has been answered fully. The Almighty has His own purposes.

— Abraham Lincoln

C onfess your faults one to another, and pray one for another, that ye may be healed. The effectual fervent prayer of a righteous man availeth much.

— *James 5:16*

Sharing builds bonds and reduces our emotional burdens. It shows our friends and loved ones how much we value them. Is there any kinder gesture than a prayer of compassion and understanding?

T hough I walk in the midst of
trouble, thou wilt revive me: thou
shalt stretch forth thine hand against
the wrath of mine enemies, and thy right
hand shall save me.

— *Psalms 138:7*

This prophetic psalm reminds us that Jesus
Christ is at the right hand of God, using our
enemies as his footstool (Hebrews 10:13).
The revival is literal, but it's also spiritual.
Repeating the verse is invigorating and
powerful.

When I was a young woman I prayed for three years that God would grant me a certain petition. Sometimes I pleaded for this as for life itself, so intensely did I want it. Then God showed me very clearly that I was praying against his will. I resigned my will to his in the matter, and a few months later God gave what was infinitely better.

— Rosalind Goforth

Likewise the Spirit also helpeth our infirmities: for we know not what we should pray for as we ought: but the Spirit itself maketh intercession for us with groanings which cannot be uttered.

— Romans 8:26

If the spirit of the ruler rise up against thee, leave not thy place; for yielding pacifieth great offences.

— Ecclesiastes 10:4

Lord, we expect to learn that "life isn't fair," but when it hurts the most is when our loved ones experience misfortune or injustice. Sometimes we try to interfere and cushion the fall but they resist and must learn for themselves in their own time. Help me to yield to your will even when I think I see the clearest path for them, and help me to welcome them back with forgiving and open arms.

My flesh and my heart faileth: but God is the strength of my heart, and my portion for ever.

— *Psalm 73:26*

Lord, I confess I feel unduly burdened at times by this pain. Some days I can barely move, and some days my heart feels sick from the sadness. Let me move with ease and grace and walk in health again. Take this yoke upon you, Lord, and help me toward my goal. I long to be released from my illness and made whole again, made free to do my best work for you. If you can nudge me in the right direction, Lord, I'll take care of the rest.

That thy beloved may be delivered: save with thy right hand, and answer me.

— Psalms 108:6

When we're waiting to make progress — a job offer, medical test, important phone call — all we can think about is the missing piece of information. Waiting to hear from God can feel the same way. We want his blessing or simply to see his work in our lives, and we must be patient.

F ollow peace with all men, and holiness, without which no man shall see the Lord.

— Hebrews 12:14

W hat God orders we must submit to uncomplainingly; but we must never submit to what God can better. Never submit to be blocked in any pious purpose or holy undertaking if, with God's help, you can roll the blocks out of your pathway.

— Theodore L. Cuyler, D.D.

B ehold, I send an Angel before thee, to keep thee in the way, and to bring thee into the place which I have prepared.

— *Exodus 23:20*

Lord, your forgiveness and love for me have transformed my life. I've been healed and liberated by fellowship and the chance to wipe the slate clean. Help me to become an extension of your love to those around me. Protect me as I learn to be vulnerable and to love my enemy as is your will. Please grant me strength. Amen.

*L*et not your heart be troubled: ye believe in God, believe also in me. In my Father's house are many mansions: if it were not so, I would have told you. I go to prepare a place for you.

— *John 14:1-2*

Blessed is the person who has steadfast and unmoving faith when everything is going wrong. That's when faith is most needed. If a person can look beyond the illusion of negative appearances and believe in a higher power at work, faith will move mountains and bring positive solutions.

We cannot tell what is for our highest spiritual good. The saving of our property or the taking it away. The recovery from sickness or the continuance of it; the restoration of the health of our loved one, or his departing to be with Christ; the removing the thorn or the permitting it to remain. He has reserved the decision, where we should rejoice to leave it, to his infinite wisdom and his infinite love.

— D.W. Whittle

*D*o all things without murmurings and disputings: That ye may be blameless and harmless, the sons of God, without rebuke, in the midst of a crooked and perverse nation, among whom ye shine as lights in the world.

— Philippians 2:14–15

Once the kids arrive, romance gets nudged aside by the carpool, and candlelit dinners happen only when the power is out. Which, we fear, God of love, could happen to us, the couple who were lovebirds once upon a time. Help us retrieve the "us" that supports the family, for we are a union blessed by you. As we cope with a full house now, remind us of empty nests ahead, a love-nest time just for us. Remind us to take a minute for ourselves amidst the loving chaos of family life.

B lessed is the man that walketh not in the counsel of the ungodly, nor standeth in the way of sinners, nor sitteth in the seat of the scornful.

— *Psalm 1:1*

Kindness, compassion, and courtesy are contagious. Be true to your faith and values in your works. Wave a car ahead of you in traffic. Ask the supermarket checker about her day. Run errands for a sick friend. The language of an open and loving heart is heard in the quietest, most simple gestures.

N ow the Lord of peace himself give you peace always by all means. The Lord be with you all.

—2 Thessalonians 3:16

The secret to happiness lies within the present moment. Only in the "here and now" will we find our life waiting to happen. Wise is the soul that cherishes this day, this hour, this moment, and does not long for other times. Fortunate is the heart that loves what is right in front of it, not what it once had or wishes it could have. And blessed is the mind that worries not over what was or what might someday be, but focuses entirely on what is.

For my thoughts are not your thoughts, neither are your ways my ways, saith the Lord. For as the heavens are higher than the earth, so are my ways higher than your ways, and my thoughts than your thoughts.

— Isaiah 55:8–9

Are you here, Lord? I've never felt lonelier than I do in this illness. When I despair, I repeat a child's prayer or familiar verse and feel soothed to connect with you. The act of praying reminds me of your presence in both sickness and health. Please help me to hold my head high so I may always feel the light of your love on my face, even in my darkest times.

L et us have grace, whereby we may serve God acceptably with reverence and godly fear: For our God is a consuming fire.

— Hebrews 12:28–29

John Donne famously used the metaphor of God as fire and wrote that God can "break, blow, burn, and make me new." We are torn down and built back up by the fire, and, like pottery, we are stronger for it.

W ait for the promise of the Father, which, saith he, ye have heard of me.

— Acts 1:4

After the most remarkable miracle of all, Jesus Christ tells the apostles that they still must be patient. In the meantime, they must be fueled by the Holy Spirit and spread the word of God. They can't guess or anticipate God's timeline.

B e perfect, be of good comfort, be of one mind, live in peace; and the God of love and peace shall be with you.

—2 Corinthians 13:11

It sometimes takes a tragic event to open our eyes to the blessings that surround us, to show us the joy in life's simple moments. Our family, friends, our neighbors, and our communities suddenly become havens of love, support, and comfort in the midst of tragedy. Wise is the person who can see the magic and wonder in simple things without having to suffer a great loss or disaster.

*B*e merciful unto me, O God, be merciful unto me: for my soul trusteth in thee: yea, in the shadow of thy wings will I make my refuge, until these calamities be overpast.

— Psalm 57:1

Why does it seem impossible to wait patiently and graciously for an overdue phone call or long-expected letter, for an ailing loved one to get better? Is there a special ingredient to speed the passage of time and relieve my burdens? Lord, please teach me to wait patiently and trust in you.

Does the prayer, "Give us this day our daily bread," mean that we are to do nothing to secure our bread, lest we show no faith in God, and simply wait in idleness for God to repeat the miracle of sending it by a raven? or, does it mean that with thankful hearts to God for the ability he has given us to work, that we go forth diligently fulfilling our task in the use of all appropriate means to secure that which his loving bounty has made possible for us in the fruitful seasons of the earth, and return with devout recognition that He is the Creator, Upholder and Giver of all, bringing our sheaves with us.

— D.W. Whittle

I s any thing too hard for the Lord?

— Genesis 18:14

W hen he hath tried me, I shall come forth as gold.

— Job 23:10

Heavenly Father, please help me realize there are different forms of healing. There are moments when life doesn't seem to change and I have to look inside to find a place of acceptance. It is in this place where I am reminded that who I am is separate from the pain that invades my life. Please help me to turn my thoughts to you. Amen.

For thus saith the Lord; Like as I have brought all this great evil upon this people, so will I bring upon them all the good that I have promised them.

— *Jeremiah 32:42*

We have countless adages about the balance of good and bad in our lives, but remember to also think about consistency. Human history is one long string of God's promises of both punishment and reward. To be reliable in your own life helps to foster the kind of trust we share with God.

L et us not fear, let us not cling to the excuses and explanations which circumstances suggest, but simply confess, "We have sinned; we are sinning; we dare not sin longer." In this matter of prayer we are sure God does not demand of us impossibilities. He does not weary us with an impracticable ideal. He asks us to pray no more than He gives grace to enable us to.

— Rev. Andrew Murray

*A*nd call upon me in the day of trouble: I will deliver thee, and thou shalt glorify me.

— Psalms 50:15

We think of God's mercy in a personal way — that he is merciful to us flawed human believers — but his mercy shines brightly each time he asks his people to spread the good word. With each new believer, God's love multiplies.

*A*nd the angel said unto them, Fear not: for, behold, I bring you good tidings of great joy, which shall be to all people.

— *Luke 2:10*

Joy reaches up in the middle of poverty to dance in the eye of a child at play. It spreads itself across the face of an old man whose illness is forgotten the moment he greets an old friend. Joy wedges itself through the cracks of loneliness when the voice at the other end of the phone line is that of someone familiar and loved. How is joy found where it is least expected? It is, no doubt, because true joy roots itself not in the shifting sands of circumstance but in the rich soil of a grateful heart.

We know how often a man may be suffering from a disease without knowing it. What he counts a slight ailment turns out to be a dangerous complaint. Do not let us be too sure that we are not, to a large extent, still living "under the law," while considering ourselves to be living wholly "under grace."

— Rev. Andrew Murray

T he Lord is my helper, and I will not fear what man shall do unto me.

— *Hebrews* 13:6

Is there a tough "worldly" problem in the back of your mind that could be solved or resolved by gathering up your courage? God is beside you. Together, you can free up that mental real estate for better uses.

I *t is true we have God's Word, with its clear and sure promises; but sin has so darkened our mind, that we know not always how to apply the Word. In spiritual things we do not always seek the most needful things, or fail in praying according to the law of the sanctuary.*

— *Henry Altemus*

C ome, and let us return unto the Lord: for he hath torn, and he will heal us; he hath smitten, and he will bind us up.

— *Hosea 6:1*

God is the beginning and the end (Revelation 22:13), and throughout Scripture we see the ways in which he is the only action and reaction. Only God can tear us, and only God can heal us. When we feel torn, there's simply no other choice than to ask God for help.

B lessed be God, which hath not turned away my prayer, nor his mercy from me.

— *Psalm 66:20*

I've set a single place at the table, O God, and am dining for the first time without my companion, my lost friend. What can we say to bless this lonely meal? What words can we use to grace this half-portion of life? Be with me as I swallow around lonely tears. Bless my remembering; inspire me to care for myself in honor of all the love that went before. May I live with this loss, always leaning on you for strength, even when I can finally stand alone.

*W*hat is the Almighty, that we should serve him? and what profit should we have, if we pray unto him?

— Job 21:15

Job uses this example to wonder why the wicked are rewarded while he is so severely punished. Eventually, Job accepts that he simply can't know why. We can never know the rest of our own stories from God's perspective, but we must know our own hearts and intentions toward God.

Come to Christ to heal you. He can in one moment make you whole. Not in the sense of working a sudden change in your feelings, or in what you are in yourself, but in the heavenly reality of coming in, in response to your surrender and faith, and taking charge of your inner life, and filling it with Himself and Spirit.

— Rev. Andrew Murray

*C*all unto me, and I will answer thee, and show thee great and mighty things, which thou knowest not.

— *Jeremiah 33:3*

God, we know that pain has produced some wisdom in our lives, but it has also created cynicism and fear. People turn on us, reject us, hurt us, and none of us wants to play the fool more than once, so we're tempted to close off our hearts to people and to you. But relationships that bring meaning and joy require vulnerability. Help us trust you to be our truest friend and to lead us to the kind of community that will bring healing rather than destruction.

Y ou thought God was to hear and
answer you by making everything
straight and pleasant — not so are
nations or churches or men and women
born; not so is character made. God is
answering your prayer in His way.

— Mary Slessor

L et every physician, before he begins
his treatment, offer up a secret
prayer for the sick person, and implore
the heavenly Father, the Physician and
Balm-giver of all mankind, to prosper
the work he is entering upon, and to
save himself and his patient from failure.

— P. W. Joyce

*A*h Lord God! behold, thou hast made the heaven and the earth by thy great power and stretched out arm, and there is nothing too hard for thee.

— *Jeremiah 32:17*

Jeremiah is a role model for how to pray in a challenging situation. He knows that God is all powerful and can't make a "bad" decision, but he is also struggling to understand the situation from his earthly perspective. Jeremiah is reverent as he opens his heart to God, and he receives a helpful, supportive answer.

B ut the fruit of the Spirit is love, joy, peace, longsuffering, gentleness, goodness, faith.

— Galatians 5:22

"Longsuffering" really sneaks in there among the fun-sounding qualities and puts a damper on things. But longsuffering can be reframed as tenacity or endurance: the strength to always keep going, to keep walking in faith, despite the obstacles and grind of daily life. The obstacles themselves will vary, but we know there will always be obstacles.

God's giving is inseparably connected with our asking. He applies this especially to the Holy Spirit. As surely as a father on earth gives bread to his child, so God gives the Holy Spirit to them that ask Him. The whole ministration of the Spirit is ruled by the one great law: God must give, we must ask.

— Rev. Andrew Murray

How shall they come to thee whom thou hast nailed to their bed? Thou art in the congregation, and I in a solitude: when the centurion's servant lay sick at home, his master was fain to come to Christ; the sick man could not.

— John Donne

For he shall give his angels charge over thee, to keep thee in all thy ways. They shall bear thee up in their hands, lest thou dash thy foot against a stone.

— Psalm 91:11–12

Why tornadoes, Lord? Why typhoons or fires? Why floods or earthquakes? Why devastating accidents or acts of terror, Lord? It's so hard to understand. Perhaps there is no way to find any sense in overwhelming circumstances. Perhaps it's about trusting in you, God, no matter what comes and leaving it in your hands, where it belongs because, in fact, you do really love us and care about us and will make things work out for us.

I n my distress I cried unto the Lord, and he heard me.

— *Psalm 120:1*

Of the many ways to suffer, I feel all of them in this firestorm of sadness. It robs my sleep, saps my strength, and changes me so much I hardly recognize myself. Ease my misery, Lord. Clear my mind as though washing streaks from a window. Hold me when I cry, releasing feelings that keep me sick; send others to hold me, too. Remind me that this pain is temporary and can be relieved, just like my worries.

At Cape May a fisherman obeyed a wholly unexplainable impulse and put back to the marshes, feeling that he had "left something," but unable to remember what it was. There he heard the cry of a lost child, wading waist deep in the incoming tide.

— Russell H. Conwell

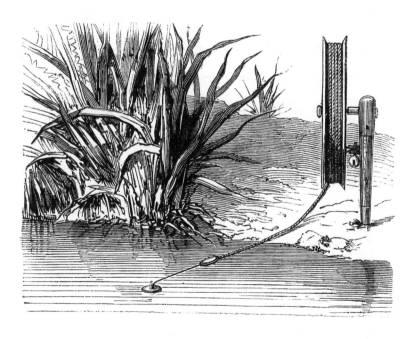

F or I know the thoughts that I think toward you, saith the Lord, thoughts of peace, and not of evil, to give you an expected end.

— *Jeremiah 29:11*

When a long-term relationship comes to an end, it's natural to mourn the loss of a companion and to grieve the death of a particular way of life. But we can mourn and grieve only for so long, then we must ask God to give us the grace and the courage to finally close that door and walk toward a new door waiting to be opened. We must take the next step God has for us. The more we seek the light, the brighter it becomes. This is God's love and compassion for us making itself known, and in his growing presence we become stronger and our faith is renewed.

The simplest, feeblest Christian can pray down blessing from an Almighty God.

— Rev. Andrew Murray

Pray for us: for we trust we have a good conscience, in all things willing to live honestly.

— Hebrews 13:18

O Lord, I have heard thy speech, and was afraid: O Lord, revive thy work in the midst of the years, in the midst of the years make known; in wrath remember mercy.

— Habakkuk 3:2

God can do anything, so Habakkuk's request for mercy is a hopeful paean instead of the difficult near-contradiction it presents to us. But to be merciful is a great blessing to both giver and receiver, a challenge worth accepting.

There is no spiritual health to be had by superstition, nor bodily by witchcraft; thou, Lord, and only thou, art Lord of both.

— *John Donne*

If I regard iniquity in my heart, the Lord will not hear me.

— *Psalms 66:18*

When you take time to "consider your ways," do you find scraps of envy or other sins that you can release from your mind? Could a loved one or friend talk them out with you? Could you share them with God and ask for his support?

May a deep sense of my ignorance, of the wonderful privilege and power of prayer, of the need of the Holy Spirit as the Spirit of prayer, lead me to cast away my thoughts of what I think I know, and make me kneel before Thee in true teachableness and poverty of spirit.

— Henry Altemus

Depend most confidently upon Him, apart from all feeling or experience. Renew that act of faith each morning, each time you pray; trust Him, against all appearances, to work in you.

— Rev. Andrew Murray

A nd the prayer of faith shall save the sick, and the Lord shall raise him up; and if he have committed sins, they shall be forgiven him.

— *James 5:15*

John Donne wrote a series of prayers as he recovered from a serious illness, each expressing his frustration and devotion to God during this time. These are among his most revered poems and include many of his most famous phrases.

*As the past has been reviewed,
and God's wonderful faithfulness
recalled, there has come a great sense
of regret that I have not trusted God
more, and asked more of him. Yes, it is
truly wonderful! But the wonder is not
that God can answer prayer, but that he
does, when we so imperfectly meet the
conditions clearly laid down in his Word.*

— Rosalind Goforth

*A*nd hope maketh not ashamed; because the love of God is shed abroad in our hearts by the Holy Ghost which is given unto us.

— Romans 5:5

Lord, the news of the world has made me a cynic. I hear myself giving up, and even bonding with my loved ones over how we've all given up. We need to stop this idle cynicism and take heart. God, you made us and you made hope for us, and there is no clearer promise than your holy word. May your love take root in our hearts and make us into better friends, neighbors, and citizens of the world.

Is there no balm in Gilead; is there no physician there? why then is not the health of the daughter of my people recovered?

— Jeremiah 8:22

Let us listen to our Lord as He offers to restore our spiritual strength, to fit us for walking like healthy, strong men in all the ways of the Lord, and so be fit rightly to fill our place in the great work.

— Rev. Andrew Murray

*L*et the word of Christ dwell in you richly in all wisdom; teaching and admonishing one another in psalms and hymns and spiritual songs, singing with grace in your hearts to the Lord. And whatsoever ye do in word or deed, do all in the name of the Lord Jesus, giving thanks to God and the Father by him.

— *Colossians 3:16–17*

My life is one long daily, hourly, record of answered prayer. For physical health, for mental overstrain, for guidance given marvellously, for errors and dangers averted, for enmity to the Gospel subdued, for food provided at the exact hour needed, for everything that goes to make up life and my poor service, I can testify with a full and often wonder-stricken awe that I believe God answers prayer. I know God answers prayer. I have proved during long decades while alone, as far as man's help and presence are concerned, that God answers prayer. It is the very atmosphere in which I live and breathe and have my being, and it makes life glad and free and a million times worth living. I can give no other testimony.

I am sitting alone here on a log. My children, whose very lives are a testimony that God answers prayer, are working round me. I am at perfect peace, far from my own countrymen and conditions, because I know God answers prayer. Food is scarce just now. We live from hand to mouth. We have not more than will be our breakfast today, but I know we shall be fed, for God answers prayer.

— Mary Slessor

I *the Lord have spoken it, and I will do it.*

— *Ezekiel 36:36*

If only we could be as consistent as God is with our own promises of punishments or rewards. Draw strength from his example!

L *et the thought that He knows my need before I ask, bring me, in great restfulness of faith, to trust that He will give what His child requires.*

— *Henry Altemus*

B ehold, at that time I will undo all that afflict thee.

Zephaniah 3 is like a play in three acts. We open on Jerusalem, a city made wretched by its worldly amorality. God describes how he'll lift the sinners out and let the righteous in, setting an example for the rest of the world. If you could "lift" a bad quality from your heart and mind, what would you choose? Could you take small steps toward this goal?

A doctor, sadly defeated in his fight for the life of his patient, went to his bedroom and prayed for light, and he "happened to think" that the patient might have swallowed some piece of metal. There was no report of the like symptoms in any case he could find in the medical books. But so deep was the impression that he secured a powerful magnet and drew forth the death-dealing needle.

— Russell H. Conwell

L et us hold fast the profession of our faith without wavering.

— *Hebrews 10:23*

There are rich rewards for believers who share their faith. Religious groups are happier and more satisfied after socializing together. Believers are more likely to give to charity, which also leads to a more satisfied and happy life.

I *wait for the Lord, my soul doth wait, and in his word do I hope.*

— *Psalm 130:5*

Help me to slow down, God of patience, because sometimes I'm so frustrated by this tough daily grind. I know you have a plan for me and I see your good works in my life and those of my loved ones. But it's hard to keep my mind clear of negative clutter when I'm in my routine, caring for my spouse or children, going to work, feeling stuck. In your word I find moments of peace, the promise of quietude.

How much our Christianity suffers from this, that it is confined to certain times and places. A man who seeks to pray earnestly in the church or in the closet, spends the greater part of the week or the day in a spirit entirely at variance with that in which he prayed. His worship was the work of a fixed place or hour, not of his whole being.

— Henry Altemus

*T*hen they cried unto the Lord in their trouble, and he delivered them out of their distresses.

— Psalms 107:6

It is easy to have self-pity and resent the painful trials and heartaches that come into our lives. But God always works for our greater good.

*A*s a large part of that intercourse between child and parent is simply asking and receiving, just so is it with us and our Heavenly Parent.

— Rosalind Goforth

*T*hou hast given him his heart's desire, and hast not withholden the request of his lips.

— *Psalms 21:2*

Bring your cool caress to the foreheads of those suffering fever. By your spirit, lift the spirits of the bedridden and give comfort to those in pain. Strengthen all entrusted with the care of the infirm today, and give them renewed energy for their tasks. And remind us all that heaven awaits—where we will all be whole and healthy before you, brothers and sisters forever.

Take courage. The burden and the agony, the triumph and the victory are all His. Learn from Him, yield to His Spirit in you, to know how to pray.

— Rev. Andrew Murray

O most mighty and most merciful God; who, though thou have weakened my bodily knees, that they cannot bow to thee, hast yet left me the knees of my heart; which are bowed unto thee evermore.

— John Donne

*F*or what thanks can we render to God again for you, for all the joy wherewith we joy for your sakes before our God; Night and day praying exceedingly that we might see your face, and might perfect that which is lacking in your faith?

— 1 Thessalonians 3:9–10

When I can see no way out of the dark tunnel of despair, my faith becomes the bright beacon of light that guides my path. When I can feel no end to the pain I am suffering, my faith becomes the soothing balm that brings relief. My faith in God never disappoints me or abandons me. Even though I cannot see it, I know it is always at work in my life.

For I will pour water upon him that is thirsty, and floods upon the dry ground: I will pour my spirit upon thy seed, and my blessing upon thine offspring.

— Isaiah 44:3

God knows of your suffering and your troubles. God knows of your sorrow and your pain. God knows you seek peace from the turmoil of life and offers you his loving presence. It costs you nothing but the willingness to accept it. It is always available, day or night, just for the asking. When life grows difficult, God's peace washes over you like a gentle and comforting rain.

We must distinguish between the will of God which is unchangeable, and His lower will which is his purpose towards us and His attitude to us. The former is unalterable; the latter varies according to the varying of our hearts. With that lower will we are called to wrestle. A man is born in poverty and obscurity, and the will of God seems to be that he should continue poor and obscure. But he wrestles with that lower will until he prevails. He ultimately moves out into the great tide of life and becomes a power. The will of God towards that man is changed.

— Norman Maclean

S *ubmit yourselves therefore to God.*
Resist the devil, and he will flee
from you.

— James 4:7

The past, O God of yesterdays, todays,
and promise-filled tomorrows, can be an anchor
or a launching pad. It's sometimes so easy to
look back on the pain and hurt and believe the
future may be an instant replay. Help us to accept the aches of the past and put them in perspective so we can also see the many ways you
supported and nurtured us. Then, believing in
your promise of regeneration, launch us into
the future free and excited to live in joy.

If at first you do not feel any special urgency or faith or power in your prayers, let not that hinder you. Quietly tell your Lord Jesus of your feebleness; believe that the Holy Spirit is in you to teach you to pray.

— *Rev. Andrew Murray*

B ut verily God hath heard me;
he hath attended to the voice of
my prayer.

— *Psalms 66:19*

Lord, it is difficult to talk about death with my
children. When friends or relatives die, my
children need to know that death is a natural
part of life; that this earthly life is not all
there is; that we will all meet again in heaven
some day. Yet the earthly loss is painful. It
causes loneliness and sorrow and sometimes
fear. These feelings can't be readily erased. My
children need to know that you are with them.
Help me to find the words that will point
them to you, Lord—words that will glorify
you, words that will soothe and take away
my children's fears. Help me to deal with the

sad feelings in tangible ways, so the sorrow is alleviated little by little. Make your presence known to each of my children in their times of need, and shelter them fromw

W hen a certain venerable minister was called on to pray in a missionary convention he first fumbled in his pocket, and when he had tossed the coin into the plate he said, "I cannot pray until I have given something." God never defaults; but He requires that we prove our faith by our works, and that we never ask for a blessing that we are not ready to labour for, and to make any sacrifice to secure the blessing which our souls desire.

— Theodore L. Cuyler, D.D.

*B*y him therefore let us offer the sacrifice of praise to God continually, that is, the fruit of our lips giving thanks to his name. But to do good and to communicate forget not: for with such sacrifices God is well pleased.

— *Hebrews 13:15–16*

The promise of hope fills the heart with a new perspective, and the eyes with a new vision. Darkness begins to lift, showing the path we could not see before, and a way out of our pain and suffering. The promise of hope opens doors we were certain were closed, and reveals solutions that evaded us. Hope is a key that unlocks the way to the blessings of God around us.

Our work for homeless children in Manchester was cradled in prayer. Every step in preparation was laid before God. But what I want specially to insist upon is the real connection there is between prayer and work. From the first my practice has been to lay our wants before God in prayer, and at the same time to use every means within our reach to obtain what we desired.

— Leonard K. Shaw

I cried with my whole heart; hear me, O Lord: I will keep thy statutes.

— *Psalms 119:145*

A heart in pain from disappointment can't always see the love that already surrounds it. That love is ever-present because it comes from God, who never abandons us. The love of God is steady and true, even when we think nobody cares about us. God does, now and forever. Opening our hearts to God is the beginning of healing, and the end of pain and suffering. God's love abides in us...always.

I t can never be wrong to ask to be made right.

— Charles Kingsley

A sk ye of the Lord rain in the time of the latter rain; so the Lord shall make bright clouds, and give them showers of rain, to every one grass in the field.

— Zechariah 10:1

Thank you, Lord, for the beauty of a rainbow. What a contrast that peaceful, glowing bow is to the tempest of the storm that came before it! Help me see rainbows as your promise to the world that beauty and happiness can come after pain and brighten my world again.

O Lord, prepare the inhabitants of the earth. To live in this world and in the world to come.

— Nancy Luce

As yet God suspends me between heaven and earth, as a meteor; and I am not in heaven because an earthly body clogs me, and I am not in the earth because a heavenly soul sustains me.

— John Donne

T rust in the Lord with all thine heart; and lean not unto thine own understanding.

— *Proverbs 3:5*

The state of hopelessness is dangerous; it is one of the worst places to allow ourselves to dwell. However, God knows our heartache, and he understands our suffering. When we have been bruised in this world, he offers us healing. We may never understand why we have to encounter heartbreaking experiences, but we can hold securely to the truth that God's justice is certain. He will heat our hearts with the flame of his joy again.

W herefore seeing we also are com-
passed about with so great a
cloud of witnesses, let us lay aside every
weight, and the sin which doth so easily
beset us, and let us run with patience
the race that is set before us.

— Hebrews 12:1

Because sin entered the world and corrupted
God's perfect design, we may find ourselves
bruised like fragile reeds by the painful effects
of a broken world. If we allow ourselves to
stay in our broken state without relying on the
powerful source of God's comfort, peace, and
love, we might even find ourselves as hopeless
as a smoldering wick about to lose its flame.

W e have read in Thy Word with what power Thy believing people of old used to pray, and what mighty wonders were done in answer to their prayers. And if this took place under the Old Covenant, in the time of preparation, how much more wilt Thou not now, in these days of fulfilment, give Thy people this sure sign of Thy presence in their midst.

— Henry Altemus

*T*hus *saith the Lord, In an acceptable time have I heard thee, and in a day of salvation have I helped thee: and I will preserve thee, and give thee for a covenant of the people, to establish the earth.*

— Isaiah 49:8

Almighty God, the world is a fearsome place where violence is glorified, disease is rampant, and young children are victimized daily. I am afraid for my family, but you are our refuge and strength, and we seek protection under the shadow of your wings (Psalm 57:1). Continue to guard my loved ones, Lord: my husband, my children, and all others so dear to me. In times of trouble, arm us for the battle and guide us safely through it. Our confidence is with you.

I *have declared my ways, and thou*
heardest me: teach me thy statutes.

— *Psalms 119:26*

There is no greater joy than being able to provide comfort to someone who is going through a rough time. Our love serves to soothe their pain, and our attention allows them to release the weight of their suffering. All we need to do is be there and listen, the way God listens to our prayers and our tears when we need comfort. We can be angels to others in need.

W hat is impossible with man is possible with God. What you see no possibility of doing, grace will do. Confess the disease; trust the Physician; claim the healing; pray the prayer of faith, "Heal me, and I shall be healed."

— Rev. Andrew Murray

*I*f ye shall ask any thing in my name, I will do it.

— *John 14:14*

In the midst of these trials, I am often ready to give up, to weep and wail over my misfortune; but you are there, Lord, to comfort me. You come to me with your healing touch to wipe away my sorrow. With your help, Father, I have so far managed to survive each trial intact, with the joy far outweighing the pain.

Christ's life and work, His suffering and death—it was all prayer, all dependence on God, trust in God, receiving from God, surrender to God. It was God's will He was come to do, and God's power He was to show forth. To pray in the Name of Christ is to pray as He prays.

— Rev. Andrew Murray

S et your affection on things above, not on things on the earth.

— Colossians 3:2

Lord, this really hurts. My heart is broken and my faith in love has been shattered. Help me find my way back to wholeness within. I know that one day I will love again, but right now, I am so angry and lost. I know that learning to forgive the one who hurt me is the fastest path to new love, but right now I need all the help I can get just to keep my chin up and my head held high. Help me heal my heart and find it even stronger than before. Help me to one day get to the point where I can forgive, find the lesson in all of this, and move on. Help me show compassion to myself and to the one who caused me this pain. Help me, Lord.

When a very little child, so young I can remember nothing earlier, a severe thunderstorm passed over our home. Terrified, I ran to my mother, who placed my hands together, and pointing upward repeated over and over again the one word "Jesus." More than fifty years have passed since that day, but the impression left upon my child-mind, of a Being invisible but able to hear and help, has never been effaced.

— Rosalind Goforth

But we will give ourselves continually to prayer, and to the ministry
of the word.

— Acts 6:4

God, I look around sometimes and see no
reason to love my life. My eyes are so often
focused on the negative things—the challenges
and obstacles and the frustrations of trying to
do the best I can all the time. Please don't ever
let me lose my ability to dig deep to that special place within where love lives. Please help
me always keep my love alive, even when I am
exhausted and defeated. Let your love remind
me that I have the choice to go a little deeper,
to move beyond the pain and the annoyances,
and to find that calm and serene well within
that never runs dry. Amen.

I pray that the last vision vouchsafed me on earth may be just that—the Saviour of men. I can then close my eyes in the knowledge that He will lead me through the dark valley that leadeth to the eternal home.

— Dr. Cameron Lees

*A*nd ye shall seek me, and find me,
when ye shall search for me with
all your heart.

— *Jeremiah 29:13*

Traumatic events leave a void in our souls that
only a closer relationship with God can fill.
By asking God to help us through hard times,
we truly come to understand that we are never
alone and that sadness is only a precursor to
joy and pain a precursor to healing.

O my Lord! strengthen my faith so in the Father's tender love and kindness, that as often as I feel sinful or troubled, the first instinctive thought may be to go where I know the Father waits me, and where prayer never can go unblessed.

— Henry Altemus

I am with you, saith the Lord.

— *Haggai 1:13*

Though you may stumble and fall along the way, God will be at your side to offer you a hand up. Though you may weep with sadness and suffer in pain, God is there to comfort you and bring healing. No matter what you are going through, God is there to help, to hold, to heal, and to love you.

D*o this, O Lord, for his sake, who knows our natural infirmities, for he had them, and knows the weight of our sins, for he paid a dear price for them, thy Son, our Saviour, Christ Jesus. Amen.*

— *John Donne*

Thou compassest my path and my lying down, and art acquainted with all my ways. For there is not a word in my tongue, but, lo, O Lord, thou knowest it altogether.

— *Psalms 139:3–4*

When we pray for healing, we pray for wholeness. Our prayers may be answered even if we don't receive exactly what we thought we asked for: The terminally ill person may be healed, yet not live; the chronically pained may still have physical suffering, yet their healing may mean they have been given an inner peace with which the physical problems are faced.

R ighteous art thou, O Lord, when I plead with thee.

— *Jeremiah 12:1*

When illness strikes, the effects go beyond the physical suffering. Fear, despair, and terrible isolation arise as the illness prolongs itself. It feels natural to lash out at your failing body, medicine that does not help, and even at the God who allowed this terrible thing to happen to you. The fate of the patient's loved ones can be equally painful, as they stand by feeling helpless to be of any real assistance. Yet, be assured that the Lord is there among you.

Beloved child of God! you know by experience how little an intellectual apprehension of truth has profited you. Beseech God to reveal Himself to you.

— Rev. Andrew Murray

I did what I was asked to do—I quietly but definitely accepted Christ as my Saviour from the power of sin as I had so long before accepted him as my Saviour from the penalty of sin. And on this I rested.

— Rosalind Goforth

W herefore I desire that ye faint not at my tribulations for you, which is your glory. For this cause I bow my knees unto the Father of our Lord Jesus Christ, Of whom the whole family in heaven and earth is named, That he would grant you, according to the riches of his glory, to be strengthened with might by his Spirit in the inner man.

— Ephesians 3:13–16

Is there anything more painful than the death of a loved one—a precious parent, spouse, friend, child? When such a loss occurs, we feel the world should stop turning; all life should freeze in its tracks, just as time seems to have stopped for us. And yet, life goes on, despite our protests. And, impossible though it seems at first, healing can and does take place. With honest grieving, understanding friends, and the passage of time, it becomes possible to cope and begin living for ourselves again. After all, it does not dishonor the dead to take care of the living, even as we treasure our memories of our lost ones.

W*e can only obtain God's best by fitness of receiving power. Without receivers fitted and kept in order the air may tingle and thrill with the message, but it will not reach my spirit and consciousness.*

— Mary Slessor

B lessed be God, which hath not turned away my prayer, nor his mercy from me.

God, shine your healing light down upon me today, for my path is filled with painful obstacles and my suffering fogs my vision. Clear the challenges from the road I must walk upon, or at least walk with me as I confront them. With you, I know I can endure anything. With you, I know I can make it through to the other side, where joy awaits. Amen.

*L*et us yield ourselves to God to obey His voice. Let no fear of past failure, let no threatening array of temptations, or duties, or excuses, keep us back. It is a simple question of obedience. Are we going to give up ourselves to God and His Spirit to live a life in prayer, well-pleasing to Him?

— Rev. Andrew Murray

Y ea, thou castest off fear, and re-
strainest prayer before God.

— Job 15:4

Thank you, Great Healer, for this second
chance at life. Forgive me for being surprised,
as if healing were beyond possibility and your
intention. Amen.

I t is not a question of what you can
do; it is the question of whether you
now, with your whole heart, turn to give
God His due, and give yourself to let His
will and grace have their way with you.

— Rev. Andrew Murray

And Cornelius said, Four days ago I was fasting until this hour; and at the ninth hour I prayed in my house, and, behold, a man stood before me in bright clothing, And said, Cornelius, thy prayer is heard, and thine alms are had in remembrance in the sight of God.

— Acts 10:30–31

Going through a difficult time alone feels like trying to find your way through a pitch-black room. The moment you reach out to another, a light appears that guides you to the other side, where the door to healing awaits.

F or whosoever shall call upon the name of the Lord shall be saved.

— *Romans 10:13*

O Lord, how it breaks my heart to see pain and loneliness in someone's eyes. Because of the unfolding of your miraculous plan to send your Son to die for us, hopelessness should never take up residence in us, Lord! We can be filled with your Spirit so quickly if we just focus on you. Help me bring your hope to those in despair, Lord.

There is a bloodless form of prayer which some use and which sends the worshipper away with an aching heart. It is the prayer that never prays directly for victory. "Thy will be done," it prays, in the spirit of submission. But prayer is not submission; it is a wrestling. In other days our fathers wrestled in prayer and prevailed.

— Norman Maclean

Our own neighbours and friends, souls intrusted to us, dying without hope! Christians around us living a sickly, feeble, fruitless life! Surely there is need for prayer. Nothing, nothing but prayer to God for help, will avail.

— Rev. Andrew Murray

*A*nd it shall be to me a name of joy, a praise and an honour before all the nations of the earth, which shall hear all the good that I do unto them: and they shall fear and tremble for all the goodness and for all the prosperity that I procure unto it.

— Jeremiah 33:9

Taking care of ourselves is the first step. Letting others care for us is the next step. But much of the journey toward healing happens when we allow God to step into our lives.

I s not Jesus Christ the same yesterday, today, and forever? Why should we wonder, therefore, at his healing touch in this age? "According to your faith be it unto you."

— Rosalind Goforth

S it thou on my right hand, Until I make thy foes thy footstool.

— Acts 2:34–35

Lord, this healing process is sometimes slow, and I get discouraged and filled with doubt. Can I take this? Will I make it? Yet you always re-mind me of your powerful presence and assure me that where I am unable to go, you will go for me and what I am unable to do by myself, you will do for me. Thank you, Lord. Amen.

"Prayer makes the darkened cloud
withdraw,

Prayer climbs the ladder Jacob saw,

Gives exercise to faith and love,

Brings every blessing from above."

— Nancy Luce

H ow precious also are thy thoughts unto me, O God! how great is the sum of them! If I should count them, they are more in number than the sand: when I awake, I am still with thee.

— *Psalms 139:17–18*

Father, you will help us to survive the seasons of surprises in our lives. For just as the harshest winter always gives way to the warm blush of spring, the season of our suffering will give way to a brighter tomorrow, where change becomes a catalyst for new growth and spiritual maturity. Amen.

O *Lord, open thou my lips; and my mouth shall shew forth thy praise. For thou desirest not sacrifice; else would I give it: thou delightest not in burnt offering. The sacrifices of God are a broken spirit: a broken and a contrite heart, O God, thou wilt not despise.*

— Psalms 51:15–17

Lord, your word created all there is. Let it now create a powerful restoration within me. Your love sustains all life. Let it now sustain and renew me. Your strength holds up the galaxies. Let it now hold me up and give me support. Your light reaches the far ends of the universe. Let it shine its healing energy upon me now. Amen.

In the day when I cried thou answeredst me, and strengthenedst me with strength in my soul.

— *Psalms 138:3*

Lord, it hurts to see those we love with tears in their eyes. We want so desperately to take away their pain and comfort them. But as we go to their sides in their time of need, we should not go alone. Only you can offer true comfort. Please add your comfort to ours as we support our friends through these trying times.